CIVIL
CAPTAIN AMERICA
WAR

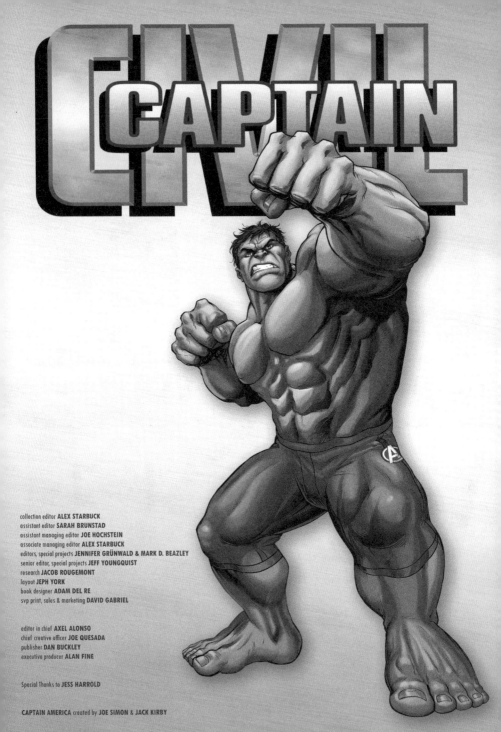

collection editor **ALEX STARBUCK**
assistant editor **SARAH BRUNSTAD**
assistant managing editor **JOE HOCHSTEIN**
associate managing editor **ALEX STARBUCK**
editors, special projects **JENNIFER GRÜNWALD & MARK D. BEAZLEY**
senior editor, special projects **JEFF YOUNGQUIST**
research **JACOB ROUGEMONT**
layout **JEPH YORK**
book designer **ADAM DEL RE**
svp print, sales & marketing **DAVID GABRIEL**

editor in chief **AXEL ALONSO**
chief creative officer **JOE QUESADA**
publisher **DAN BUCKLEY**
executive producer **ALAN FINE**

Special Thanks to **JESS HARROLD**

CAPTAIN AMERICA created by **JOE SIMON & JACK KIRBY**

MARVEL UNIVERSE CAPTAIN AMERICA: CIVIL WAR (SCHOLASTIC EDITION). Contains material originally published in magazine form as MARVEL ADVENTURES SUPER HEROES (2008) #12; MARVEL ADVENTURES IRON MAN #9; AVENGERS: EARTH'S MIGHTIEST HEROES #1; MARVEL UNIVERSE AVENGERS: EARTH'S MIGHTIEST HEROES #6, #8 and #12; MARVEL ADVENTURES SUPER HEROES (2010) #17; and AVENGERS VS. #1. First printing 2016. ISBN# 978-1-302-90077-9. Published by MARVEL WORLDWIDE, INC., a subsidiary of MARVEL ENTERTAINMENT, LLC. OFFICE OF PUBLICATION: 135 West 50th Street, New York, NY 10020. Copyright © 2016 MARVEL No similarity between any of the names, characters, persons, and/or institutions in this magazine with those of any living or dead person or institution is intended, and any such similarity which may exist is purely coincidental. **Printed in the U.S.A.** ALAN FINE, President, Marvel Entertainment; DAN BUCKLEY, President, TV, Publishing and Brand Management; JOE QUESADA, Chief Creative Officer; TOM BREVOORT, SVP of Publishing; DAVID BOGART, SVP of Operations & Procurement, Publishing; C.B. CEBULSKI, VP of International Development & Brand Management; DAVID GABRIEL, SVP Print, Sales & Marketing; JIM O'KEEFE, VP of Operations & Logistics; DAN CARR, Executive Director of Publishing Technology; SUSAN CRESPI, Editorial Operations Manager; ALEX MORALES, Publishing Operations Manager; STAN LEE, Chairman Emeritus. For information regarding advertising in Marvel Comics or on Marvel.com, please contact Jonathan Rheingold, VP of Custom Solutions & Ad Sales, at jrheingold@marvel.com. For Marvel subscription inquiries, please call 800-217-9158. Manufactured between 10/13/2015 and 11/21/2015 by HESS PRINT SOLUTIONS, A DIVISION OF BANG PRINTING, BRIMFIELD, OH, USA.

10 9 8 7 6 5 4 3 2 1

AMERICA WAR

writers
SCOTT GRAY, ROGER LANGRIDGE, FRED VAN LENTE, CHRISTOPHER YOST, ELLIOTT KALAN, PAUL TOBIN, ROB WILLIAMS, JOE CARAMAGNA & CHRISTOS GAGE

pencilers
MATTEO LOLLI, CRAIG ROUSSEAU, GRAHAM NOLAN, PATRICK SCHERBERGER, CHRIS JONES, MARCIO TAKARA, AMILCAR PINNA, TIM LEVINS & DARIO BRIZUELA

inkers
CHRISTIAN VECCHIA, CRAIG ROUSSEAU, VICTOR OLAZABA, PATRICK SCHERBERGER, POND SCUM, MARCIO TAKARA, AMILCAR PINNA, KARL KESEL & DARIO BRIZUELA

colorists
SOTOCOLOR, MARTE GRACIA, JEAN-FRANÇOIS BEAULIEU & DARIO BRIZUELA

letterers
DAVE SHARPE, VC'S CLAYTON COWLES & JOE CARAMAGNA

cover artists
CLAYTON HENRY & GURU-eFX, TOMMY LEE EDWARDS, SCOTT WEGENER & JEAN-FRANÇOIS BEAULIEU, KHOI PHAM WITH EDGAR DELGADO & PETE PANTAZIS, BARRY KITSON & VAL STAPLES, AND KALMAN ANDRASOFZKY

assistant editors
NATHAN COSBY, MICHAEL HORWITZ, ELLIE PYLE & MARK BASSO

consulting editor
RALPH MACCHIO

editors
NATHAN COSBY, MARK PANICCIA, TOM BRENNAN, RACHEL PINNELAS & BILL ROSEMANN

senior editor
STEPHEN WACKER

collection cover artists
TODD NAUCK & RACHELLE ROSENBERG

IN 2016, MANY OF EARTH'S MIGHTIEST HEROES ARE ON A CINEMATIC COLLISION COURSE IN MARVEL'S *CAPTAIN AMERICA: CIVIL WAR* — with Cap and Iron Man leading the charge! But before the battle lines are drawn, join the movie's biggest stars in this collection of some of their most exciting adventures. The Sentinel of Liberty takes top billing — including in a wartime mission with his best buddy, Bucky — and Shellhead grabs his share of the limelight. But fear not, there's still room for plenty of scene-stealing by more of your favorite Avengers — such as Black Widow, Hawkeye, Falcon, Black Panther and the Hulk! They'll face foes including Hydra and M.O.D.O.K. in titanic tales of team-ups and takedowns that can be enjoyed by anyone, of any age, time and again. It's all-out action for all comers, and now it's all yours!

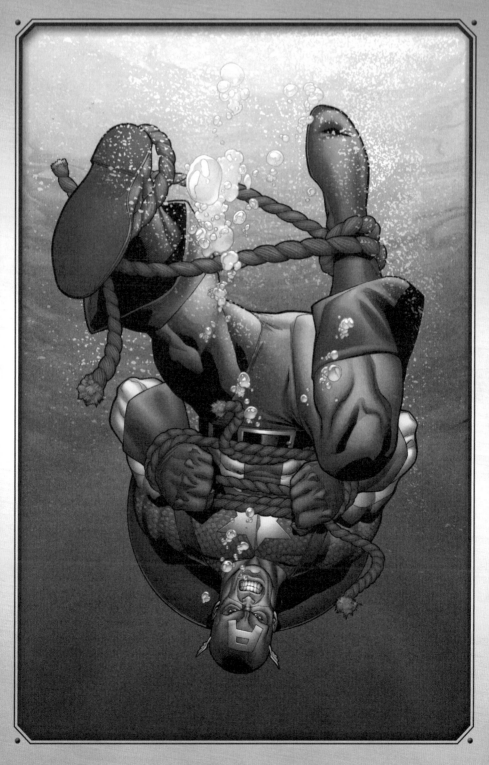

MARVEL ADVENTURES SUPER HEROES #12

...and the main story this week remains *Captain America*. A figure identical to the living legend of *World War II* was sighted four days ago in *New York* battling the terrorist group *Hydra*.

The entire nation is buzzing with speculation...

SCOTT GRAY WRITER

DAILY BUGLE

WHO IS THE NEW CAPTAIN AMERICA?

MATTEO LOLLI PENCILER
CHRISTIAN VECCHIA INKER

FRIENDSOFCAP.COM

CAP IN ACTION IN CENTRAL PARK!!!

VIDEO TUBE

SOTOCOLOR COLORS
DAVE SHARPE LETTERER
HENRY & GURU COVER
JOE SABINO PRODUCTIC
RALPH MACCHIO CONSULTING

Hey, you can laugh all you *want*, man, it don't matter to me! The real Cap's *totally back!*

NATHAN COSBY EDITOR
JOE QUESADA EDITOR IN CHIEF

DAILY BUGLE

FAKE CAPTAIN AMERICA GOES ON RAMPAGE!

DAN BUCKLEY PUBLISHER
ALAN FINE EXECUTIVE PRODUCER

I saw Cap in action in 1943! I'm tellin' you straight, the guy I saw in Central Park was the *same fella...*

JOE VANDERBILT – WORLD WAR II VETERAN

THE NATIONAL SPECULATOR

CAPTAIN AMERICA IS A MARTIAN SPY!

STEVE ROGERS WAS TRANSFORMED INTO THE ULTIMATE SUPER-SOLDIER IN WORLD WAR II. NOW REBORN IN THE MODERN AGE, HE FIGHTS FOR JUSTICE AS **CAPTAIN AMERICA**

WEB OF DECEIT

Panel 1:

Man, the world won't *shut up* about you, Steve! You're bigger than Brangelina!

I wonder why the government hasn't confirmed my identity to the public...?

It's called "plausible deniability," dude--they're scared you're gonna *embarrass* them! I mean, *think* about it...

...what if you started hosting *American Idol?*

Panel 2:

See *this?* That *S.H.I.E.L.D.* babe Sharon Carter gave it to me. "You're the Captain's *official* liaison, Jones," she said... "I'm expecting regular email reports on his behavior!"

Guess I'd better keep my nose clean!

Panel 3:

C'mon, let's grab a coffee...

¿Sigh¿... y'know, Rick, in *my* day, people came to cafes to *talk.* Is *everybody* in America addicted to this "televideo" nonsense?

That's "television," dude, and this is even *better!* Steve Rogers: Meet the *internet!*

Panel 4:

We're talking about *millions* of *computers* all around the *world*, all *linked up*, all sharing *important info!*

So I see...

"100 Stupidest Poodle Tricks"...

Panel 5:

Okay, so it ain't all *Shakespeare!* It's still a great way to dig up facts. It's like the world's biggest *library*...

Fine, I'll give it a try. Let's ask your internet something *useful*... What does it know about *Hydra?*

Panel 6:

SPARROW HAWK
SEARCH ENGINE

HYDR

No problemo! We start with a *search engine.* This one gets the fastest results...

Paper! **Paper!** Getyamornin' paper!

Here ya go, mister! The first one's on the house--or the Home Page!

Hey, wasn't that...

"Hydra Boy." Looks like he's more than just a *cartoon*...

THE HYDRA GAZETTE

DINOSAUR FOUND IN ATLANTIC!

Very funny.

Hey, look at that lazy, long-haired *beatnik!*

You're a *weirdo!*

We don't want *your* kind here!

The natives are getting *ugly,* Rick...

Move it!

Soon...

We've lost them...

Okay, what's the deal here? One second we're looking at that *website,* and then--*pow!* We're in a *Happy Days* episode!

Keep your head, Rick, we--

Wh--?!

Yeee-Harrr!

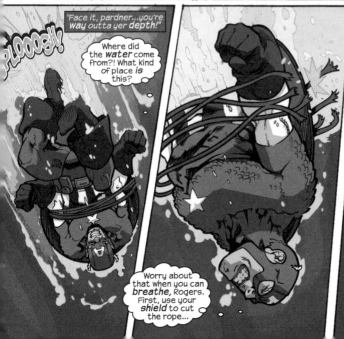

Looks like Hydra Punk decided I wasn't gonna be a *problem*--he's left me *alone*. Big mistake, kid--nobody knows the web better than *Rick Jones!*

Okay, if everything inside this website is *real*, then I'll have to *navigate* the *pages*. That means I need...

...a menu, please!

Here ya go, honey!

It all looks *great*, babe--I think I'll start with the *Message Board*...

HOME
QUIZ
MERCHANDISE
SPORTS
GALLERY
F.A.Q.
LINKS
MESSAGE BOARD

Now where have I ended up? Looks like an *arena...*

...get ready to *rummmble!*

In the *green* corner, it's that sensational streak of success, *Hydra Boy!*

In the *red-white-and-blue* corner, it's that lethargic *Living Legend, Captain America!*

He's reached the *Sports Page,* ladies and gents! And you know what *that* means...

GO, HYDRA BOY!

BOO CAP!

DING DING

Wa-hoooo! We made it!

Head for S.H.I.E.L.D., Rick! *Good work!*

So long, suckers!

Later...

Captain America...has *escaped* the digital trap, Supreme One.

The failure was *mine*. I...I take *full responsibility.*

I offer *my life*-- to restore the honor of *Hydra.*

Did we obtain the data we required?

Y-yes, Supreme One. Everything we needed...

Then there was *no* failure, my son. Be at *peace.*

Everything is going according to *plan...*

Now *that* has got to be one of the *strangest* things I have ever seen.

Hey, Cap-- I don't think it's after the guys! Did you notice how it's blasting kind of *randomly*?

Randomly... or at something we haven't *noticed* yet! Let's take it down! Maneuver 29-B!

Right behind you!

Durchlauf! Laufen Sie für Ihre Leben, kleine Flöhe!

ZZAPP!

Get that, Chalky! This is *dynamite!*

Nawww! I only do babies, weddings and *bar mitzvahs!*

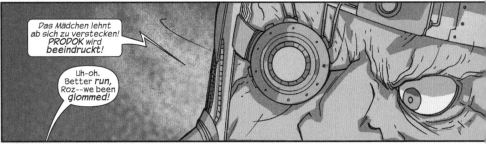

Das Mädchen lehnt ab sich zu verstecken! PRODOK wird beeindruckt!

Uh-oh. Better *run*, Roz--we been *glommed!*

Jetzt laufen Sie! Jetzt Sie Fell!

KPOW!

Nice knowing you, Chalky!

Pleasure's all mine.

Surprise.

Was geschieht--?

SMASSH!

NEIN!!

The End.

MARVEL ADVENTURES IRON MAN #9

ILLIONAIRE INVENTOR
ONY STARK BUILT A SUIT
F ARMOR THAT SAVED
S LIFE. HE NOW FIGHTS
GAINST THE FORCES OF
VIL AS THE INVINCIBLE
RON MAN!

THE BUNKER

FRED VAN LENTE WRITER
GRAHAM NOLAN PENCILER

VICTOR OLAZABA INKER
MARTEGOD GRACIA COLORIST
DAVE SHARPE LETTERER

TOMMY LEE EDWARDS COVER
ANTHONY DIAL PRODUCTION
NATHAN COSBY ASST. EDITOR

MARK PANICCIA EDITOR
JOE QUESADA EDITOR IN CHIEF
DAN BUCKLEY PUBLISHER

...I don't know quite how to *tell* you this, S.E.R.V.A.C....

...but there was never any "Great Cataclysm."

The world's still *spinning*, history keeps marching *on*...

LIES! LIES! LIES!

That is illogical!

What We're Surviving For...

Our *files* show all the *signs!* Society's *morals* were *degenerating!*

The *environment* was on the brink of *collapse!*

Wars threatened to tear the world *apart!*

There is *no other reason* S.E.R.V.A.C. would be entrusted with this duty!

Okay, now I *know* you're simply reflecting the paranoia of your *creator*, Obadiah Stane--

That is *not* the Programmer's designation.

Our Programmer was *Stark-comma-Howard!*

Howard--?! Is he *down* here? Is he who you're protecting?

That could explain *everything!*

"Everything I've ever *wondered* about since the day I came home from my freshman year at *M.I.T.*"

Jarvis! What's *happened?* Why are there so many *reporters* out front?

I-I'd best let your *mother* explain, young master Anthony...

Mom!

What's *wrong?*

Your father has *abandoned* us, Tony! He cleaned out the contents of our family's *safe-deposit boxes* and *disappeared!*

And the *accountants* tell me our company *finances* are a *disaster!* We're on the brink of *bankruptcy!* I don't know what we'll *do!*

Don't *cry*, Mom--I'll leave *school*--I'll turn the company around...

...somehow...

"And I *did* turn it around, thanks to my *inventions.*"

"But not without *two years* of *sleepless nights* for Mom and me."

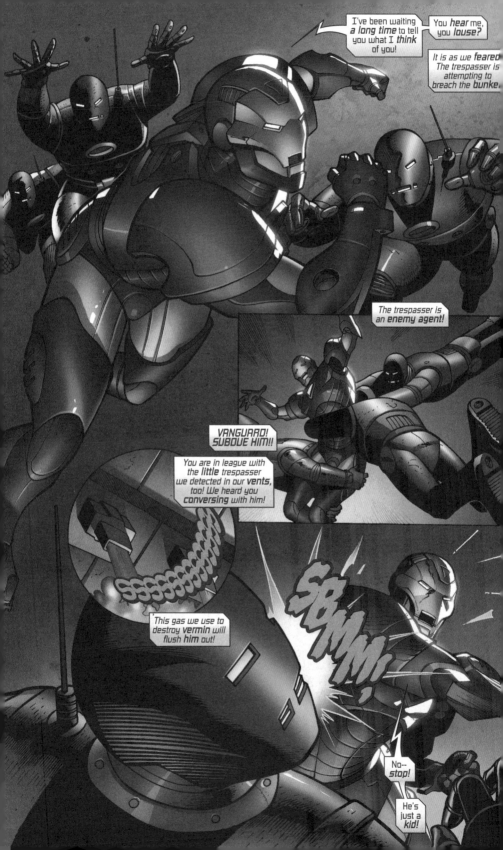

Look, Eli! I'm not one of those robots!
I'm human, just like y--
S.E.R.V.A.C. REMAINS UNDEFEATED!
WE CAN TRANSMIT OUR MIND INTO ANY OF OUR VANGUARD!
S.E.R.V.A.C. IS MANKIND'S LAST HOPE! WE WILL NOT FAIL IN OUR MISSION!
JAMMER: ON
S.E.R.V.A.C. is an obsolete and neurotic pile of transistors and vacuum tubes!
My advanced armor can jam any transmission S.E.R.V.A.C. wants to make!
FZZZZRRRR
Your vanguard is based on a design I created when I was seven years old!
You see, Dad? You see how far I've come?
And how WRONG you WERE--
Halt program!
Trespasser: your designation is Stark-comma-Anthony?
You are the Programmer's son?

KLIK KLIK KLIK KLIK

THUNK

HISSSSSSSS

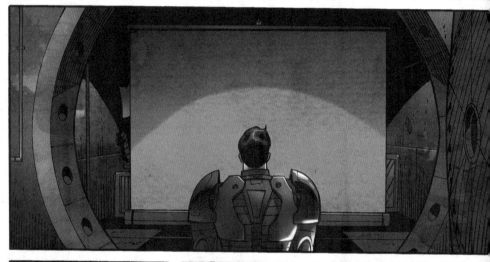

RRAAAATTTLE

Hello.

My name is Howard Stark.

I have no idea who or even when anybody will be watching this.

AVENGERS: EARTH'S MIGHTIEST HEROES #1

TRUST ME.

TRUST
CHRISTOPHER YOST WRITER
PATRICK SCHERBERGER ARTIST
JEAN-FRANÇOIS BEAULIEU COLORIST
DAVE SHARPE LETTERER
TAYLOR ESPOSITO PRODUCTION
MICHAEL HORWITZ ASSISTANT EDITOR
NATHAN COSBY EDITOR
JOE QUESADA EDITOR IN CHIEF
DAN BUCKLEY PUBLISHER
ALAN FINE EXECUTIVE PRODUCER

END.

MARVEL UNIVERSE AVENGERS:
EARTH'S MIGHTIEST HEROES #8

COME ON, LET ME SMASH THEM.

WE HAVE BUT EIGHT MINUTES TO REACH THE ROOF, WE CANNOT RISK REVEALING OUR PRESENCE.

I WILL HANDLE THEM.

UNH!

YOU SEE? *STEALTH* AND *SPEED*.

REAL *IMPRESSIVE*, FANCY FEAST. DON'T EVEN KNOW WHY I'M HERE.

DO NOT TAKE THIS IN THE WRONG SPIRIT, HULK, BUT YOU WERE NOT *MY* FIRST CHOICE FOR THE MISSION.

I ONLY SAY THIS IN THE CAUSE OF *OPENNESS* AND *HONESTY*.

YOU'VE GOT A REAL *POLITE* WAY OF INSULTING A GUY.

WELL, I *AM* ROYALTY.

HOW COULD I FORGET? YOU MENTIO IT EVERY FIFTEEN MINUTES.

SEVEN MINUTES. AND TWENTY MORE FLOORS STILL TO *CLIMB*. WE MUST *RISK* THE ELEVATORS.

HAVE YOU GOT A SCREW LOOSE?! YOU'RE *NOT* SQUEEZING ME IN THAT *TIN CAN!*

HAWKEYE APPRECIATES *STEALTH*, BUT HE'S UNDERCOVER IN THE RINGMASTER'S *CIRCUS OF CRIME.*

BLACK WIDOW IS AN INFILTRATION EXPERT, BUT SHE'S SHUTTING DOWN THE TASKMASTER'S SUPER VILLAIN ACADEMY.

IT'S LIKE YOU *WANT* ME TO SMASH YOU.

DING

ANT-MAN AND WASP ARE IDEAL FOR *QUIET* RAIDS, BUT THEY'RE DISARMING COUNT NEFARIA AND MADAME MASQUE.

WHOA!

PLEASE LET ME TAKE THESE GUYS OUT.

NO NEED!

OOF!

NUMBER 407, WHO WAS IN THE ELEVATOR?

FALSE ALARM. AN AUTOMATIC PROGRAM, *NOTHING* MORE.

SIX MINUTES. WE MUST MOVE *FASTER*, PLEASE TRY TO KEEP UP.

OKAY, THAT'S IT, PUSS N' BOOTS. I DON'T CARE ABOUT ANY MADBOMB.

I'M MAD ENOUGH RIGHT NOW!

RAAR!

AND THAT'S THE *END* OF THIS LITTLE *JOY BUZZER.*

BETTER CHECK ON *SYLVESTER.*

IS THAT ALL? SURELY YOU CANNOT HAVE GIVEN UP! WHO ELSE IS PREPARED FOR ANNIHILATION?!

SNAP OUT OF IT, GARFIELD. MINDLESS VIOLENCE IS MY THING, YOU STICK TO *"STRATEGY"* OR WHATEVER.

HULK? THANK YOU. I AM AFRAID I LOST CONTROL OF MYSELF.

REGARDLESS, THE CITY IS *SAVED.* BY WORKING TOGETHER AS A *TEAM,* WE STOPPED THE THREAT OF THE *MADBOMB* WITHOUT DOING *DAMAGE* TO THIS *MAGNIFICENT* STRUCTURE.

WELL... NOT *TOO MUCH* DAMAGE, ANYWAY.

MARVEL ADVENTURES SUPER HEROES #17

writer PAUL TOBIN • artists MARCIO TAKARA & AMILCAR PINNA • colorist SOTOCOLOR • letterer DAVE SHARPE
production MANNY MEDEROS • cover artists BARRY KITSON & VAL STAPLES • editor RACHEL PINNELAS • senior editor STEPHEN WACKER

ONE MONTH AGO, SHE *SAW* SOMETHING.

IT WAS IN AN ALLEYWAY, IN DRESDEN.

SHE *SAW US!*

LINNETTE: CLASSIFIED AGENT

SHE *ESCAPED* BY SWIMMING THE RIVER *ELBE* IN THE MIDDLE OF THE NIGHT.

TWO WEEKS AGO, SHE WAS IN ROME.

ANY LUCK? HAVE WE *FOUND* HER?

WE'RE CLOSING IN. WON'T BE LONG.

ONE WEEK AGO, THEY *ALMOST* HAD HER.

AND NOW *WE* HAVE HER.

WE'RE TOO LATE. WE'LL HAVE TO ASK OUR MASTER WHAT HE WANTS US TO DO.

UNITED STATES EMBASSY

HOPEFULLY HE WON'T BE TOO...ANGRY.

AND *SINCE* WE HAVE *LINNETTE*, WE HAVE TO *PROTECT* HER. THAT'S *YOUR* JOB.

WHEN IT COMES TO THE *SPY GAME*, THERE AIN'T *NOBODY* BETTER QUALIFIED THAN *THE BLACK WIDOW*.

COLONEL NICK FURY: HEAD OF *S.H.I.E.L.D.* (STRATEGIC HAZARD INTERVENTION ESPIONAGE LOGISTICS DIRECTORATE)

NATASHA ROMANOFF: THE *BLACK WIDOW*: WORLD'S # 1 SPY

YOU'RE GOING TO BE HER BODYGUARD UNTIL SHE CAN TESTIFY AT...AT A MEETING YOU'RE NOT CLEARED TO KNOW ABOUT.

GREAT. *SECRETS.*

YOU *KNOW* HOW MUCH I LOVE THEM.

NOW, WE DON'T HAVE MUCH TIME. I'VE GOT A *SUPERSONIC PLANE* WARMING UP THAT WILL...

SO... WHAT DID THIS WOMAN *SEE?*

AGAIN, I CAN'T TELL YOU. YOU DON'T HAVE THE *SECURITY CLEARANCE.*

NICK, *MY* CLEARANCE IS HIGH ENOUGH TO STROLL INTO THE *OVAL OFFICE* AND SEARCH THROUGH THE PRESIDENT'S DESK DRAWERS.

SO TELL ME WHAT'S GOING ON.

SORRY, NATASHA. NOT THIS TIME.

THAT'S *IT,* THEN. *HIDING* HASN'T BEEN WORKING. IT'S TIME FOR A *POWER PLAY.*

OLD TOWN SQUARE. PRAGUE. 8:12 PM.

"I...I *RESPECT* YOUR KNOWLEDGE OF THE SPY GAME, BLACK WIDOW, BUT I'M *NOT* POSITIVE THIS IS THE BEST IDEA."

SOMETIMES THE *BEST* WAY TO PLAY YOUR CARDS IS TO *SHOW* THEM ALL. WE'VE BEEN OUTMATCHED IN TERMS OF *SECRECY.* OUR OPPONENT KNOWS OUR EVERY MOVE.

SO...WE'LL LET *EVERYONE* KNOW OUR EVERY MOVE.

WHOEVER *"HE"* IS...IF HE WANTS TO KIDNAP YOU *NOW...* HE'LL HAVE TO DO IT IN FULL VIEW OF THE WORLD, NOT BEHIND CLOSED DOORS.

NO. *OH NO!* HE'S *HERE!*

WELL, *GOOD,* THEN I'LL *FINALLY* SEE THE MAN I'M UP AGAINST.

SO, IT'S YOU.

DOCTOR DOOM. RULER OF LATVERIA.

SUSPECTED, LET'S SAY *HEAVILY SUSPECTED*, OF A GREAT MANY CRIMES AGAINST, WELL, EVERYONE.

AND YET, HERE WE ARE ALL TOGETHER IN OLD TOWN SQUARE. AND I'M NOT SURE *WHAT* YOU'RE TRYING TO COVER UP, *WHY* YOU'VE BEEN TRYING TO KIDNAP THIS WOMAN, BUT...

...EVERYTHING'S *PUBLIC* NOW, AND IF YOU TAKE HER *NOW* IT BECOMES A BIGGER PROBLEM THAN *WHATEVER* ONE YOU'RE TRYING TO DEAL WITH.

HMMPFF.

IF YOU EVER NEED A *JOB*... CALL ME.

IF *YOU* EVER NEED A *JAIL CELL*, CALL ME.

HMMM?

OH. YOU.

HOW DID YOU GET PAST ALL THE...? NAWW. NEVER MIND. I SHOULD JUST...

NICK...YOU WANTED ME ON THAT JOB BECAUSE I'M THE WORLD'S GREATEST SPY, BUT YOU WOULDN'T TELL ME *ANYTHING.*

LISTEN...IF YOU *EVER* DO ANYTHING LIKE THIS AGAIN...IF YOU *EVER* SET ME UP AGAINST A *MYSTERY* THAT TURNS OUT TO BE SOMETHING LIKE *DOCTOR DOOM...*

...THEN I JUST WANT YOU TO KNOW THAT IT *ISN'T* A MYSTERY HOW I'M GOING TO *REACT.*

I'M GOING TO BE THE *BLACK WIDOW.*

AND I'M GOING TO BE *MAD.*

THE END.

MARVEL UNIVERSE AVENGERS:
EARTH'S MIGHTIEST HEROES #6

GRAHAM BELL ISLAND.
KARA SEA. RUSSIA.

REPEAT! S.H.I.E.L.D. HELICARRIER, WE ARE LOSING POWER!

HEAVY ICE BUILDUP! WE'VE LOST PART OF A WING!

UM...

SUPERFAST MACH 10 QUINJET PROTOTYPE.

HE JUST SAY WE LOST A WING?

FREAKING OUT A LITTLE HERE.

WE ALL ARE, BROTHER.

EXCEPT HER.

THE BLACK WIDOW. YOU DON'T WORRY ABOUT ICE WHEN YOU'RE THAT COLD ALREADY.

SHE'S RUSSIAN, RIGHT? THINK SHE CAN SEE HER OLD HOUSE FROM HERE?

'ERYONE AND OUT, H.I.E.L.D. 'ROOPS! NOW!

THIS BIRD IS GOING DOWN, SO WE ARE GO FOR IMMEDIATE EXIT!

THAT MEANS WE'RE CRASHING! USE 'EM OR LOSE 'EM!

ABSOLUTE ZERO

WILLIAMS WRITER
TIM LEVINS PENCILS
KARL KESEL INKS
SOTOCOLOR COLORS
VC's CLAYTON COWLES LETTERS
KHOI PHAM & EDGAR DELGADO COVER ART
E PYLE EDITOR
TOM BRENNAN EDITOR
STEPHEN WACKER CHILLY
AXEL ALONSO EDITOR IN CHIEF
JOE QUESADA CHIEF CREATIVE OFFICER
DAN BUCKLEY PUBLISHER
ALAN FINE EXEC. PRODUCER

YOU KNOW WHY WE'RE HERE! HYDRA ARE EN ROUTE AND COULD BE ON SITE ALREADY!

SO OPEN YOUR CHUTES AS LATE AS POSSIBLE AND DON'T GIVE THEM A FLOATING TARGET!

THIS IS THE ARCTIC CIRCLE, PEOPLE! WE ARE ON OUR OWN! BACKUP IS COMING, BUT IT WILL NOT GET HERE IN TIME!

HIT WATER THROUGH THE ICE AND THOSE SPECIAL SUITS YOU'RE WEARING WILL PROTECT YOU FOR TWO MINUTES MAX, THEN YOU DIE!

CAPTAIN, THIS PLACE WAS A *TOP SECRET* SOVIET MILITARY AIRFIELD IN THE COLD WAR. *DEATH* IS ALL IT HAS EVER OFFERED.

TWO MINUTES IS ALL I WILL NEED.

EARLIER.

IT'S CALLED THE *ZEROBOMB.* ARTEM FEDOSEEV BUILT IT DURING THE 1960S. WOULD'VE DESTROYED SEVENTY-FIVE PERCENT OF AMERICA WITH *ONE* WARHEAD.

THE SOVIETS WERE GOING TO TEST IT NEAR *GRAHAM BELL ISLAND* WHEN *FEDOSEEV* WAS OVERCOME BY *GUILT* AND *FEAR* FOR WHAT HE'D CREATED.

HE STOLE, HID AND BURIED THE PROTOTYPE SOMEWHERE BENEATH THE ICE AND WAS NEVER HEARD OF AGAIN.

THE SOVIETS NEVER FOUND IT. OR HIM.

FEDOSEEV LEFT A LETTER WITH ONE OF HIS ASSISTANTS DETAILING THE ZEROBOMB'S LOCATION. THE ASSISTANT REVEALED THIS ON HIS DEATHBED. YESTERDAY.

THE LOCATION OF THE ZEROBOMB IS NOW *OUT* IN THE OPEN, AND YOU *KNOW* WHAT THAT MEANS...

CHUTE!
I SEE A CHUTE!
WOW, THAT
WAS LATE!

HAVE REACHED
TARGET. ZERO COVER
DOWN HERE. WE'RE
SITTING DUCKS.

HAWKEYE,
THE CANNON.

PIECE
OF CAKE.

I REALLY
CAN'T FEEL MY
HANDS.

YAAAAAHH!

ANNNND...
CHUTE OPEN!

OKAY,
THAT WAS...

CLOS...
WHOA!

A... SUBMARINE?

GUESS NOW WE KNOW *WHAT* FEDOSEEV HID THE *ZEROBOMB* IN, HUH?

WHAT ARE YOU *WAITING* FOR?

DON'T YOU *RECOGNIZE* A RIDE HOME WHEN YOU *SEE* ONE?

BADDA-BADDA-BADDA

STOP THEM! THEY'RE GETTING AWAY!

STOP THEM!

HATCH *SEALED*. TEAM OKAY?

ALL ACCOUNTED FOR.

I DIDN'T KNOW YOU COULD *DRIVE* A SUBMARINE.

MY LIFE AS A SPY...MUCH WAS *ORDERED* OF ME...

LUCKY FOR ALL OF US, HE *REFUSED.*

HE DISCOVERED HE HAD MORE TO OFFER THE WORLD THAN JUST DEATH.

THEY ORDERED FEDOSEEV TO DO ALOT OF *THINGS*, TOO.

AVENGERS VS. #1

BROS BEFORE FOES

JOE CARAMAGNA-WRITER   DARIO BRIZUELA-ARTIST
VC's JC-LETTERER   MARK BASSO-ASSISTANT EDITOR   BILL ROSEMANN-EDITOR
AXEL ALONSO-EDITOR-IN-CHIEF   JOE QUESADA-CHIEF CREATIVE OFFICER   DAN BUCKLEY-PUBLISHER   ALAN FINE-EXEC. PRODUCER

RRRRRRRRR

IT WASN'T AN E.M.P. THEY BLASTED YOU WITH...IT WAS *MALWARE.* IF YOU *POWER DOWN,* YOUR BUILT-IN ANTI-VIRUS SOFTWARE WILL ISOLATE IT SO IT CAN BE *PURGED!*

HMM. I HADN'T THOUGHT OF THAT. EVEN IF YOU'RE RIGHT, IF I POWER DOWN, I'LL BE *COMPLETELY DEFENSE-LESS* FOR A WHILE. I WON'T STAND A CHANCE!

IF YOU *DON'T,* I'LL *NEVER* GET YOU OUT OF HERE *ALIVE.* YOUR ARMOR'S NOT COOPERATING.

DO IT! I'LL KEEP THIS THING BUSY WHILE YOU REBOOT. TONY, *PLEASE...*

...YOU SAY I'M AN AVENGER, BUT AT SOME POINT YOU'LL HAVE TO *TRUST* ME LIKE ONE.

... FINE.

VZZT

FOR BOTH OF OUR SAKES YOU'D BETTER BE RIGHT.

YOU! YOU DID THIS! I DON'T KNOW *HOW*, BUT--

TA-TA! CALL ME WHEN YOU CHANGE YOUR MIND, M.O.D.O.K.

FOOSH

YOU INFECTED MY ARMOR WITH A VIRUS. NOT *COOL*.

FOR THAT...

?

...I THINK YOU ALL DESERVE A *TIME-OUT!*

FWASH

KLANGG

NEITHER OF US CAN HOLD A CANDLE TO CAP WHEN IT COMES TO COMBAT STRATEGY, BUT, HEY, THIS *WORKED*.

NO. *ONE* OF US CAN.

I DON'T SAY THIS *OFTEN*, AND IF YOU TELL ANYONE I'LL *DENY* IT, BUT--

I WAS *WRONG* TO RUSH IN LIKE THAT.

WE'RE *TEAMMATES. EQUALS*. FEEL FREE TO POKE ME THE NEXT TIME I TREAT YOU AS ANYTHING LESS. NOW...

...GO SWEEP THE PLACE FOR MORE *A.I.M. GOONS* WHILE I CALL NICK FURY.

≈AHEM.≈

OH, HEH. *SORRY.*

I'LL SWEEP THE PLACE FOR GOONS, AND *YOU* CALL NICK FURY...

...AVENGER.

THE END

MARVEL UNIVERSE AVENGERS: EARTH'S MIGHTIEST HEROES #12

YOU CAN'T BE *TOO* SMART IF YOU DON'T KNOW I CAN *ABSORB* YOUR ANDROID'S ENERGY...

...AND GIVE IT *RIGHT BACK!*

FWASSHH

ANALYSIS: THE THINKER'S EGO REQUIRES THAT HE BE THE SMARTEST MAN IN ANY ROOM.

THAT IS WHY HE DOES NOT GIVE HIS ANDROIDS THE ABILITY TO THINK FOR THEMSELVES.

AND WHY THEY WILL ALWAYS BE INFERIOR TO ONE WHO *CAN.*

ERROR-- ERROR-- FZZTT

THAT THE *"WEAKLING SCIENTIST"* YOU'VE DISMISSED AS POWERLESS--

--WAS TRAINED TO FIGHT BY CAPTAIN AMERICA!

WHAM

WHICH HELPS AGAINST A PUDGY LAB RAT. AGAINST *THAT*--

--NOT SO MUCH.

WHAKOOOM

SYSTEM ERROR-- VIBRATORY DAMAGE TO HARD DRIVE--SAFETY SHUTDOWN--

THE AVENGERS CAME HERE TO *SAVE* ME.

SO I HAVE TO DO WHAT I CAN TO *SAVE* THEM...

...WITH WHATEVER'S AVAILABLE.

CLICK

YES!

RRAAGH

--UHH. DID I--HURT ANYONE--?

EASY, CAP. EVERYONE'S FINE.

FOR THE MOMENT. THE THINKER'S MACHINE IS OVERLOADING WITH GAMMA ENERGY, AND ONLY HE KNEW HOW TO STABILIZE IT.

GIVEN TIME, I COULD FIGURE IT OUT, BUT WE ONLY HAVE SECONDS.

THEN WE HAVE TO GET OUT OF HERE!

THERE'S NO TIME. THAT GAMMA ENERGY HAS TO GO SOMEWHERE, AND WE BOTH KNOW WHERE.

BRUCE, ARE YOU SURE?

I AM. DO IT!

RRRAAAAA!

THE MACHINE'S MELTED. WE CAN'T CHANGE HIM BACK.

HULK...DO YOU KNOW US? WE'RE YOUR FRIENDS.

OBSERVATION: THAT DID NOT WORK SO WELL THE LAST TIME.

FRIENDS...?

YES.

HULK KNOWS WHO HIS FRIENDS ARE.

BRUCE, IF YOU STILL WANT TO BE FREE OF THE HULK, I CAN ASK IRON MAN TO TRY TO RECREATE THE MAD THINKER'S MACHINE.

NO, THAT'S OKAY. I THINK YOU WERE RIGHT, CAP. THE PROBLEM WASN'T THE HULK...IT WAS *ME*.

I WAS SO BUSY FEELING SORRY FOR MYSELF THAT I *GAVE UP*, WHEN I SHOULD HAVE BEEN GLAD THE HULK IS DOING GOOD WITH THE AVENGERS INSTEAD OF CAUSING TROUBLE.

I'M STARTING A NEW RESEARCH PROJECT TODAY. IF I'M NOT HELPING THE WORLD ONE WAY, I'LL BE HELPING THE OTHER.

WELL, THAT'S GOOD. BECAUSE YOU DEFINITELY MAKE A BETTER HULK THAN I DO.

AND I THINK I'LL LEAVE THE SHIELD-SLINGING TO YOU. THAT THING'S *HEAVY*.

OH, YOU HANDLED IT PRETTY WELL WHEN YOU HAD TO.

AFTER TODAY, CAP...

...I KNOW I CAN HANDLE *ANYTHING*.

CAPTAIN AMERICA

IN 1940, AS AMERICA PREPARED FOR WAR, a frail young man volunteered for an experiment that transformed him into the ultimate physical specimen. As **CAPTAIN AMERICA, Steve Rogers** fought the good fight until a freak mishap placed him in suspended animation for decades. When he awakened, Rogers was truly a man out of time, though no less committed to fighting the evils of this perilous new era.

IRON MAN

INVENTOR. BUSINESSMAN. LADIES' MAN. SUPER HERO. Gravely injured and kidnapped during what should have been a routine weapons test, billionaire genius **Tony Stark** saved his own life by designing a life-sustaining shell —— the high-tech armor that is the invincible **IRON MAN**. A modern-day knight in shining armor, Stark faces corporate intrigue and super-powered menaces —— both alone and alongside his fellow Avengers.

BLACK PANTHER

WITH THE SLEEKNESS OF THE JUNGLE CAT whose name he bears, **T'Challa** — king of Wakanda — stalks both the concrete city and the undergrowth of the veldt. So it has been for countless generations of warrior kings, so it is today, and so it shall be — for the law dictates that only the swift, the smart and the strong survive. Noble champion. Vigilant protector. **BLACK PANTHER**.

BLACK WIDOW

NATASHA ROMANOFF IS AN AVENGER, an agent of S.H.I.E.L.D. and an ex-KGB operative. As an enemy agent, the femme fatale tangled with a number of heroes — including Iron Man, Hawkeye, Nick Fury, Spider-Man and Daredevil. Now, the **BLACK WIDOW** uses her amazing acrobatic abilities and fearsome fighting skills for good.

FALCON

TRAINED BY CAPTAIN AMERICA, and serving as his longtime ally and fellow Avenger, **Sam Wilson** is the high-flying hero of the people known as the Falcon. Motivated by a strong sense of community and accompanied by his falcon Redwing, the **FALCON** focuses his efforts on making a positive difference in the world.

HAWKEYE

ATTEMPTING TO EMULATE IRON MAN
by donning a colorful costume and employing
his archery skills to fight crime, circus performer
Clint Barton was mistaken for a super villain.
When he revealed his true intentions to the
Avengers, Iron Man sponsored his membership
on the team. The world's greatest archer lives life
on the edge, straddling the fine line between right and wrong.
Heroes are expected to play by the rules, and **HAWKEYE** does
— his own.

HULK

**CAUGHT IN THE HEART OF A NUCLEAR
EXPLOSION**, victim of gamma radiation gone
wild, **Dr. Robert Bruce Banner** now finds
himself transformed during times of stress into
the dark personification of his repressed rage
and fury — the most powerful man-like creature
ever to walk the face of the Earth, the strongest
one there is, **the INCREDIBLE HULK**.

BUCKY / WINTER SOLDIER

**CAPTAIN AMERICA'S SIDEKICK JAMES
"BUCKY" BARNES** died in action in the closing
days of World War II, only to be resurrected by
Department X, the Soviet Union's Secret Science
Division and brainwashed to be their perfect
Cold War assassin: **the WINTER SOLDIER.** But
when his former partner saved him and restored his memories,
his troubles truly began. Haunted by his past, **Bucky Barnes**
fights for redemption in the present day.